THE COURAGE CHRONICLES

DRAGON'S SONG

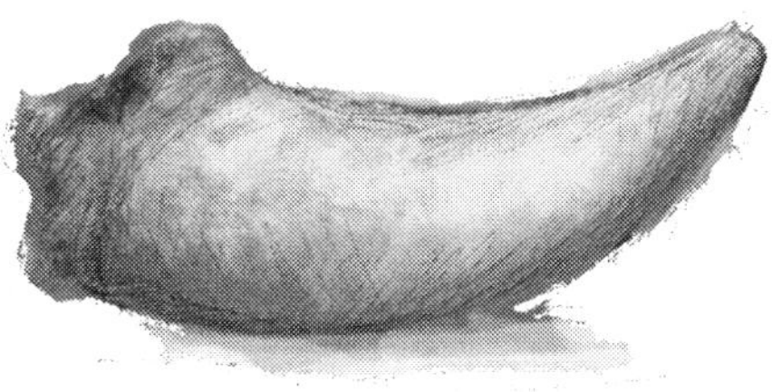

Laurie Wright
Jennifer Stables

Definitions:
Solis means Sun
Selene means Moon
Lux means light
Nox means night

Published by Jenny Dale Designs

For information regarding permissions contact
Jenny Dale Designs:

www.JennyDaleDesigns.com

ISBN:978-0-9958047-7-7

ISBN-13:978-0-9958047-7-7

Dedication

For the inspiration to write a better book for younger kids, thank you Paisley. For the character inspiration, thank you to my kids, Sebastien, Elise and Max (who does really like to give hugs and kisses!) ~Laurie

To James and Myles, you are the magic in my life! ~Jennifer

CHAPTER ONE
A NEW TREASURE

"Stop, drop and roll!!!" Sebastien fell into the pile of leaves and rolled from side to side. He was pretending that he had been set on fire by a fearsome dragon. His little brother Max immediately dropped into the pile of leaves beside him and started rolling around gleefully. He jumped on top of his big brother, forgetting that he was supposed to be the fearsome dragon who was setting things on fire!

Elise stared at her brothers for a few seconds with squinted eyes and a pouting mouth. She was annoyed. Why were they having fun playing in the leaves they'd all

just raked up, while she was still working? Their game looked too fun to ignore for long, though, so decided to join them instead of feeling annoyed.

"Make way for the bravest unicorn EVERRRRRRR!!!!" she yelled as she leaped into the pile. "I'll get you, you fierce dragons!!!" They were rolling around the leaves, throwing them at each other, and pretending to be fantastical creatures fighting one another. Their neat and tidy leaf pile was now scattered around the yard.

"Attention all messy animals!" yelled their mom from the kitchen window. "You have 10 more minutes until bath time, and Max, you're first. Clean up the yard now, kids."

Right away Max dove into the leaf pile and tried to hide from helping, and Elise loudly announced that she had to pee (a classic move every 6 year old knows). Sebastien groaned to himself, annoyed that once again most of the cleaning would be left to him... AS USUAL. At 9 ½ he was the oldest kid in the family, and most of the time the clean up jobs fell on him (which he hated). Just because he was the oldest, shouldn't mean that he had to do all of the work! He poked around the leaves where Max was hiding, hoping to prod him out. But it wasn't working, and Elise was already starting to head into the house.

Sigh.

I'll trick them into coming *closer*, Sebastien thought, *then I'll grab them and force them to help.*

"Oooo, look at this cool rock!! WOW!!" His voice was was loud and exaggerated as he pointed to the ground, pretending to see something. He widened his eyes and hung his mouth open in surprise. "This is the COOLEST rock I've ever seen! You two should really come over here and…." his voice trailed off and stopped.

Sebastien crouched down towards the ground where he had been pointing. At first he was just pretending to see something cool, but then he *actually* spotted something really cool! What seemed to be a strange, pointed, white rock was sticking out of the ground. He quickly forgot about tricking the other kids and started digging. The further he dug, the bigger the rock seemed to get! He wrapped his hands around it and pushed it from side to side, leaning his entire body onto it to help loosen it from the ground. Elise and Max came right over and got down on the ground with him, curious about what he'd found. Sebastien's trick had worked, but he didn't even care anymore.

"What is it?" Elise asked.

Max repeated the question, in his three year old way, "IS it???"

"I think it's a rock, but it's the weirdest rock I've ever seen!" Sebastien was still working hard to dig it out, but was getting

closer to freeing it. Finally he pulled out a large, white, jagged rock– about the length of his longest finger.

"There!" He held it up for close inspection.

"Toof!" exclaimed Max, as he jumped up and down excitedly. He recognized what the strange rock was immediately. It wasn't a rock...it was a tooth! An exceptionally big tooth!

Sebastien and Elise sat back on their bottoms and stared at the large tooth in silence. Similar thoughts were going through both their minds. *What kind of animal had a tooth that big!? And when had it been in their backyard!!?*

Their mom called to them again to give them the five minute warning. They were startled out of their daze and starting to move again. "Let's put this in our suitcase", Sebastien said to Elise.

The three children ran into the house and

down the stairs into the basement. A month ago they had discovered a very old (and very cool) mysterious suitcase among the moving boxes. It was now the place where they kept every new and interesting treasure they found. They raced over to behind the bookshelf where they'd hidden it out of sight. Sebastien and Elise pushed the locked suitcase towards Max– he was really good at unlocking things!

The kids heard the familiar popping sound of the suitcase being unlocked. They opened it slowly, taking a moment to ponder the faded pictures of horses on the outside of it. The smell of the suitcase was strange yet oddly familiar– kind of like the smell of the large, old books at the library.

Sebastien reached towards the pocket inside the suitcase, ready to place the tooth inside. Then he paused. He turned the tooth from side to side, inspecting it from every angle. The wide end, where it had been attached to some giant creature's mouth, was jagged and rough. The outside of the tooth was really smooth, just like his own teeth. At the pointy end there was a small hole leading to the inside of the empty tooth. It made the tooth look like a whistle. Sebastien couldn't help himself...he put the tooth in his mouth and blew into it.

Unexpectedly the noise that came out was a haunting melody, beautiful and moving, not like a whistle at all. Suddenly, from the wide end of the tooth a powerful light began to shine. It was so bright that it lit up the entire basement. The children looked away from the tooth, closed their eyes, and shielded them with their hands.

~CHAPTER TWO~
LOST AGAIN

The kids peeked out from behind their fingers. This event was all too familiar to them and they wondered where they might be when they opened their eyes this time. As they moved their hands away from their faces and blinked their eyes, their jaws dropped open. They looked up, up, UP at a very loud, very big waterfall! Water cascaded over the top of a cliff, roaring as it crashed its way to the bottom. There, the water continued rolling along on its journey, swelling up into white waves, then calming down and becoming a peaceful stream. It gently curved from side to side before

turning around a corner and flowing out of sight.

The children looked down at their feet. They were standing on a sandy beach beside the bottom of the waterfall. They glanced at the waterfall. It was so big they couldn't see the top from where they were standing, only the white swells of the water as it came crashing down.

A strange noise caught Max's attention, and he wandered over to a pile of rocks to his left to see what was making it. Still in awe of the magnificent waterfall, Sebastien and Elise barely noticed him go. They were mesmerized by the motion of the water and the loud noise it made.

Max peeked behind the pile of rocks. Sitting there was a strange little animal, roughly the same size as Max. He held out his hand to the little guy and gave him a big smile. Just as he was about to give him a hug and a kiss, Max noticed the animal's pointy teeth

and long, sharp claws. He took a step back, still looking at the animal.

The baby smiled back at Max and jabbered something that Max couldn't understand. This made Max like his new friend even MORE!! Who needs real words? The two started running around the rocks, laughing together and playing. An interesting little bug that was hopping about caught their attention. They immediately started following it to see what it would do and where it would go next.

Elise thought back to their last experience– when they'd been magically transported to a land filled with unicorns. Max had run off then, and she figured she'd better make sure that didn't happen again. She turned to tell Max to stay close by, when she spotted him playing with what looked like a little dragon. They were running in circles, chasing the bug they had found.

“Sebastien! SEBASTIEN!!!” she loudly whispered, pulling at his arm and pointing towards the two littles. “Is that what I think that is??!” Her mouth hung open and her eyes were wide as she processed what she was seeing.

Sebastien looked over where Elise was pointing and stumbled backwards a bit in shock. *A dragon?*! Max had found, and was playing with, a small dragon with shiny red, almost mirror-like, scales. It had short arms and legs, with sharp claws, and pointy teeth, that were impressive for a little dragon. They were having fun, watching a bug jump on the ground and Max didn’t seem to be in any danger. The dragon was just a baby having fun too. Both older children let out a sigh, as they realized Max was in no danger from this little guy.

A loud splashing noise from the direction of the waterfall drew their attention quickly away from their brother. Turning to see what was causing the noise, they saw a fully grown dragon fly smoothly out from behind the waterfall. Soaring on large, powerful wings, it flew up into the sky and looked around. Then it flew down to the beach where it hovered above the shore in front of them.

Elise and Sebastien drew in deep breaths and quickly stepped backwards until they were up against a large boulder and couldn't move any further.

The dragon's wings were spread wide and strong, flapping to hold it steady in the air as it looked from side to side as though it were searching for something. The children were awestruck. They'd seen plenty of dragons in movies and TV shows, and read about them in books. They were usually described as fearsome and angry, breathing fire on anything that dared to cross their paths. This dragon however, was not like that. It wasn't angry looking and breathing

fire in all directions. It wasn't baring its teeth and trying to eat everything in sight. If anything this dragon seemed sad. Its eyes were worried and it was frowning.

The kids studied its golden scales, and the shell-like plates on its back. It had wide set wings running from its shoulders to its hips. Its large eyes were green like emeralds. It's head was covered in a hard, smooth shell that almost looked like a helmet or a crown. After about a minute, the dragon flew up into the sky and away from the falls. Sebastien and Elise stared at the dragon disappearing from sight and let out the breath they'd been holding in. Then they both started talking at the same time.

"That was a dragon! A BIG dragon!" Sebastien spoke slowly and his jaw was hanging open in shock and awe.

"HOLY MOLY, that was a real dragon!" Elise spoke quickly and hopped up and down with excitement.

"Did you SEE that?!" Sebastien looked at Elise to make sure he wasn't dreaming.

"What was it looking for?" Thinking about how it had seemed to be looking for something, Elise was curious.

At her last question, both kids went still. Instantly they both had a good idea of what the dragon was looking for.

"Max!" they bellowed at the same time, turning to look at him. But Max and the baby dragon were no longer there.

CHAPTER THREE
TOOTH TO THE RESCUE

"Oh no, we lost him again!!" wailed Elise. How could they lose Max again? Thankfully last time he disappeared in a new land he had a unicorn keeping him safe and looking after his well-being. But this time he had wandered off with a dragon! A baby dragon, sure, but still a dragon!

Sebastien regained his composure and took charge. "We have to find him!" He set off towards the nearby woods, expecting Elise to follow him, which she did.

They had only walked a short distance before Elise stopped in her tracks. "Do you hear that?" Sebastien paused to listen.

Sure enough an enchanting sound began to grow around them. It was a song– more beautiful than anything they had ever heard before. The voices lifted in song were getting louder, and the words were so enchanting the children closed their eyes and swayed on their feet.

The song paused, and the children opened their eyes to see dusk beginning to fall. They took a few steps away from the cover of the trees to see if they could spot whomever was singing. Their eyes fell on the most incredible sight– six dragons were flying above the waterfall in a circle. Their heads were lifted towards the sky and mouths were open in song.

Glorious moon of silver light,
Keeper of our sacred night;
With your power and your glow
Command the water's ebb and flow.
The day has passed and Sun now sleeps
While creatures seek the watch you keep.

It was mesmerizing. Their voices intertwined in perfect harmony, their words carrying over the noise of the waterfall and drifting through the air, as the moon rose. A magical spell was being woven over the entire land, and as the moon got higher in the sky the soothing lullaby was putting all the world to sleep, including them.

Just as Elise and Sebastien were about to close their eyes and nod off, they heard a rustling in the trees around them. Something was there… something big… and it seemed to be getting closer!

"Nox!! Where are you! Nox, this isn't funny!" A desperate voice was calling, growing louder and closer. The kids nervously stumbled backwards away from the voice, unsure of who, or what, it belonged to. Despite their fear, they were too sleepy to run away.

The sound of rustling leaves and breaking branches grew louder and louder until...

CRASH!

A dragon burst from the bushes and stopped right in front of Sebastien! It had thick, shiny scales ranging from yellow, to orange to red, like fire. Its body was thin, with long arms and legs.

Gasping for air, Sebastien stumbled backwards, tripping on a rock and falling onto his bottom. The dragon stopped short and stared at the children, surprised. She quickly regained her composure though, and asked, "Did you see Nox? I can't believe I lost him again! I am going to be in SO much trouble!!"

"Who are you?" Elise summoned up enough courage to speak to the enormous creature.

"My name is Lux. Nox is my baby brother...and he's LOST!!"

Abruptly the enchanting song that had almost put them to sleep changed. Above them, the moon had stopped rising. In front

of them, the crashing waves in the water had stilled to such a calm state that the entire lake looked like glass.

There was still a group of dragons high in the sky, but now two of the dragons were missing. The other four dragons were still singing, but the song seemed less powerful. It didn't sound as beautiful as it once had. The dragons that remained in the sky started thrashing their necks back and forth. Their singing turned to cries of desperation. They were clearly upset.

As Sebastien and Elise watched the dragons, they began to understand why they were singing. The song commanded the moon– it was clear now that it was supposed to, but without all six of the dragons singing, the song didn't seem to be working. They watched as the four flying dragons became more agitated and distressed.

In desperation Lux, the dragon, moved to the edge of the water and lifted her head up to the sky. She began to sing, joining with the others in song, but her efforts didn't seem to be enough. The moon had stopped in its tracks and wouldn't rise any higher.

Without thinking, Sebastien pulled out the tooth he'd found in his yard and blew into it, like a trumpet. It made a wonderful, deep and rich sound, that spiralled up and into the sky and joined with the voices of the other dragons. With Lux and Sebastien's help, the dragon's finished their song. Their flying appeared calmer. Sebastien lowered the tooth, while gazing at the sky. Lux moved to stand beside him.

Everything was silent. The river and the lake were perfectly still, reflecting the sky and the moon like a mirror. The roar of the waterfall had completely faded away. The water cascading down the cliff, forming the beautiful waterfall, now hung off the rocks like an enormous, liquid glass curtain. It was as though time had stopped.

It was clear that Sebastien and Lux had helped prevent a crisis of some sort. They had helped the flying dragons complete their song, but something still wasn't quite right.

A great gust of wind suddenly blasted them, and pushed down on the group of three. Two dragons flew down towards them, using their great wings to slow them down, and then to land. Jaws gaping open, eyes as large as dollar coins, the kids watched as the two magnificent dragons set down directly in front of them.

CHAPTER FOUR
A TRANSFORMATION

Sebastien and Elise felt no danger from the huge creatures. It was clear that these dragons were not angry– they were worried. The kids recognised one of the dragons. It was the gold one who'd flown out through the waterfall earlier. The other dragon had red scales so dark they were almost black. They were shiny, and there were ridges on his back. His wings were so large they covered the entire span of his body, from his head to his toes.

"Lux!" called the distraught, gold dragon. "Where is your brother?" She was speaking directly to the dragon that was standing beside Sebastien. “Your father and I tried to sing the sacred moon song but we could not finish it. We were just too upset once we saw that Lux was not with you! Now look what has happened!”

She motioned towards the sky where the moon hung above the horizon. A strange, erie darkness filled the sky– not quite the darkness of night, but not the brilliance of day. “The moon has not fully risen because your father and I could not finish the song!” The distress this dragon was feeling was obvious, and the children realized she was the mother of the missing baby dragon.

“Selene, it will be okay, we’ll find him soon enough. Lux, tell us what happened.” Calmly, this dragon tried to reassure Selene, however he was also quite upset. His worried eyes were a dark, shiny green and he was staring imploringly at Lux, seemingly unaware of the human children who were there too.

Her words came out in a rush. "We were playing, he was hiding, and then he was just gone! I noticed right away, I swear, and I've been looking all over for him, ask them!!" Lux was talking in a hurry, trying to defend herself, but she sounded guilty anyway.

Selene let out a small growl, snorted, and fire came out her nostrils! Elise and Seb both yelped, surprised and frightened by the fire. At the sound of their yelp, the adult dragons turned their heads and stared at them. They didn't seem surprised by the sight of humans in front of them, and briefly Sebastien wondered if people came here everyday.

"I am Solis, and this is Selene." said the father of the baby dragon. "We thank you for joining in to the song. Because of you all is not lost, yet. Nox, our smallest child, is a joy in our lives. Unfortunately he is also a constant worry since he gets lost so often. We were overcome with concern and unable to continue singing when we saw he was no longer with Lux."

Lux hung her head with guilt at her father's words.

"You must help," Selene demanded. She rose up high and stood stiffly, her hands wringing in front of her. Her eyes looked at them, and then quickly towards the woods that surrounded them. She couldn't help searching for her baby, and she kept snorting bits of fire from her nose. "We have to find Nox, but we must also sing to command the moon down, at daybreak. I can not sing if my child is not found, but I can not abandon the song! I do not know what to do!!" Her voice was getting higher and her fire snorting was more frequent. It was clear she would not be able to sing the sacred song in this state.

Solis made a decision. He said firmly to Selene, "We will go look for him, and we will find him." Then turning to Sebastien he said, "You must join with the other dragons, and complete the circle if we are not yet back." To Lux, he said, "Do not feel badly. He has wandered away often enough and we have always found him. It will be alright. Stay with this boy and teach him to fly."

Then Solis looked towards the sky at the other dragons. He opened his huge jaws and began to sing. A mournful array of notes floated up to the sky. Like a gust of wind, the other four dragons swooped down and formed a circle around Sebastien. Surrounded by six large dragons, who were all staring at him in silence, he began to tremble.

Solis spoke with authority to the other dragons, "Selene and I have let you down. We were distracted and distraught. We couldn't finish our part of the song. But this boy is the one who joined in our song, acting purely on instinct. If it wasn't for his and Lux's quick thinking and intervention the moon would have fallen from the sky! But

we still need him. He will have to complete the circle and sing with you tonight if we are not yet back by daybreak." The others all bowed their heads in agreement. They turned to Sebastien, and started walking towards him.

What was happening??

They opened their mouths and roared at Sebastien.

Holy moly, they were going to eat him!

Glowing, blue fire sprayed out of their giant gaping mouths and completely washed over Sebastien. Panicked, he quickly dropped to his knees and curled up into a ball, sure he was about to be eaten or burnt to a crisp. It was obvious he was done for.

It was over in an instant. Somehow, he had not become food, burnt or even slightly singed. The fire must have been magical because he wasn't hurt at all (although he did feel warm). His skin felt warmer than usual, and it itched like crazy. The itching moved from the outside of him inward. The magic fire was crawling inside his body, itching its way right to his core. Where it had felt warm a few seconds before now felt cool and hard.

Sebastien's head was spinning with the heat. He was so woozy that he thought he might fall over. His body felt 100 pounds heavier and he was having trouble holding up his head. It felt like a bowling ball perched on his neck! Then he caught sight of himself in the still water at the edge of the beach. He gasped in disbelief and stumbled backwards. He tripped on his tail - *he had a tail!* - and fell over awkwardly. The magical fire that hadn't harmed him...it had transformed him. ***He was a dragon!!***

CHAPTER FIVE
TO COMMAND THE MOON

Elise was torn. She didn't know what she should do.

Clearly, Sebastien needed help. He had transformed into a dragon just seconds before, and was kind of freaking out. But he wasn't hurt, or in pain. He was just a dragon now. Elise knew exactly how he felt. A few weeks ago Elise had been magically transformed into a unicorn. Yes, it was strange and somewhat scary, but she was okay. She knew Sebastien would be okay too...as soon as he got used to it!

Elise was more worried about Max right now. He was alone in the woods with a baby dragon and two grown dragons tracking him down! Max was going to be more than freaked out, he was going to be terrified when he saw those two, even though they *seemed* nice enough. And Max was only two years old (well, almost three)– still pretty little to keep calm at the sight of huge, upset dragons!

A choice had to be made: which brother should she help?

Elise had changed over the past month. She felt more confident since her experience as a unicorn. She made decisions more easily and didn't second guess herself. Now she also knew she was capable of handling anything that were to happen, magical or otherwise. Elise knew this situation would require her to be very brave. She took a big gulp before walking over to her big brother.

She knelt beside Sebastien who was sitting down, staring dumbfounded at his new tail.

“Sebastien, you’re going to be okay. They said you must join in the song to command the moon, and you need to learn to fly to do it. But you have wings now! Did you see them? Lux will stay with you, and help you figure things out.” She looked up to Lux for confirmation, and the dragon nodded in agreement. “I HAVE to go after Max. He’ll be scared when they find him, and he’s still so little. I hope you understand. I’ll be back as soon as I can!” Elise hugged his rough arm and shoulder a bit, patted his cheek and its new hard skin, and then stood up.

“You’ll take care of him, right?” she demanded of the dragon she faced.

Lux nodded again, and said to Elise, “Go help our little brothers, he’ll be okay here with me.” She inclined her head towards Sebastien as she said it.

With a deep breathe out, and one last, long look at Sebastien (who was now trying to look over his large dragon shoulders to see his wings) she ran in the direction that the babies and the grown up dragons had gone.

Thoughts of little Max being scared at the sight of the dragons helped Elise run faster than she ever had, on two feet anyway. There was a good trail, possibly from the massive dragons forging it ahead of her, so she was able to cover a lot of ground quickly. The tree leaves created a canopy above that blocked out almost all light. As she moved farther into the forest, it became darker and darker, and Elise could no longer run for fear of tripping on downed branches and exposed tree roots. She had to slow right down and watch where she was stepping very carefully.

She caught up to Selene and Solis after what seemed like forever (but was likely about ten minutes). They were walking slowly with their faces down near the ground, searching for clues of the little ones.

Furrowed brows, tears and fire snorts told the story of frustration without any words.

They both looked up at Elise as she approached, and then Selene sat down and let out a huge sigh. “It is too hard!” she wailed. “The tracks make no sense, it is like they wove in and around every flower and every rock, and then their trail just disappears. We might NEVER find them!!”

Solis sighed as well, and went over to console her. Elise felt badly for the parents of the little dragon, who clearly thought the situation was desperate. She tried to make them feel better by sharing the tale of her last adventure.

“Last month, we thought we would never find Max when he wandered away from us. Well, he actually wandered up a rainbow! One minute he was there, next he was gone, just like that!” Elise told the story of how Max had caused quite a commotion with the unicorns, and about how in the end he had turned up okay– safe and sound, and happy.

Selene's tears had stopped and she had hope in her eyes now. "That was SO brave of you! You remind me of our Lux, she is courageous too. Did she tell you the story of what it is we do?"

"I heard the beautiful singing and I think that your song has something to do with the moon not fully rising and the way the water is now?" Elise tilted her head to one side and waited for Selene to explain.

"Yes. We dragons command the moon with our song. Our job is to make sure it rises in the evening, and falls at dawn. We sing so that the moon comes, which is incredibly important." She looked questioningly at Elise, asking if she knew why the moon was important. Elise shrugged her shoulders to indicate that she did not, in fact, know why the moon was so important.

Solis stood up and started looking at

the footprints again, trying to figure out the direction the little ones had gone.

Selene was grateful for the distraction and perked up, excited to tell her story. "The moon is so important because it has a special power: gravity. Without the moon's gravity in the right spot, pulling on the earth, the water becomes still. If it does not rise fully, it also affects the sun cycle which would make for shorter, colder days and put all life in danger. Even one night without the moon rising can alter the water and the length of days, here and in your world as well."

Elise had grown still listening to Selene talk, and was eager to hear more, "I never thought about the moon much before. I didn't realize how important it was!" She sat staring at the dragon, hoping she would keep talking.

Selene did. "Dragons have been granted the most beautiful singing voices as a reward for accepting responsibility for this important task. There are only a few of us, and each is required to sing or else the moon will not fully rise, as you see has happened tonight." She hung her head down, looking ashamed at having caused the problem tonight. "Our Nox is so special to us, we were certain he would have the best voice in the group! Even if he does not, it would be okay. He makes us laugh all the time– he is so funny. He is just a baby...how will he survive out here in the woods? Soon the song must be sung, the moon must fall, and Nox must be found!" She was getting distraught again and at that, Selene stood up and walked to where Solis was looking closely at the ground.

Had he found something?

CHAPTER 6
TRICKY TAIL

"I. Have. A. TAIL!" Sebastien was hopping around, trying his best to see more of the tail that felt so strange, that was attached to his backside and that dragged around behind him, heavily. Sebastien had transformed into an amazing purple dragon. He had wings (WINGS!) that rose out from his body and then bent, like an elbow, and hung down to his knees. He had spikes on the top of his head that were a darker purple than his body, and the scales on the front of him shimmered, a shiny, silvery purple. He was gorgeous, not that he could really appreciate it. It was hard to get used to the weight distribution of this new body. His head was heavier and his wings were light, but he couldn't quite work them right yet. His tail dragged along behind him, like a very long sock attached to the back of a belt and filled with rocks.

His new friend Lux was laughing at him, so hard in fact that she was having a difficult time catching her breath. "You are SO funny!! It's like you've never had a tail before." Delighted at her cleverness, she howled with laughter again, and then had a coughing fit that ended with a puff of smoke and fire coming out of her nose. "Okay, you need to learn how to fly. Can you at least stand up now?" She put her hands on her hips impatiently as Sebastien tried to stand on both legs, balance his wings and not trip on his tail.

Sebastien– the dragon– managed to stay upright and move closer to where Lux was waiting. He was a bit wobbly but he was starting to get the hang of it.

"Of course I can stand, and I'm sure I can fly." he boasted to Lux.

Sebastien usually assumed he could do anything he tried with little difficulty. He was the oldest, the strongest, the fastest, and he always expected to be the best. Clumsily he began to run along the beach. Lifting his wings ready to soar... he tripped on his tail and fell on his face. Lux bit her lip, trying really hard not to laugh and make him feel badly. If she made fun of him he might give up, and it was so important that he learn to fly!

"It's okay, just try it again, it takes a long time to learn, I'll be amazed if you ever do, actually."

Sebastien was determined to prove himself, and continued to run and jump and flap his wings furiously, only to flop face first down in the sand, over and over and over again. After so many fails, he rolled over

onto his back - difficult with a tail - and stared up at the moon, hovering in the wrong spot.

"I don't understand why the moon is so important, anyway. The sun is what is MOST important, it gives us warmth and light. What does the moon do for us?" Sebastien scowled and squinted his eyes and challenged Lux about the dragon's important job.

"Seriously?" She looked at him in disbelief for a minute and then let out a big sigh. Maybe explaining it to him would motivate him to try flying again. "You know what tides are, right? How the ocean rises and falls a couple of times every day?"

He nodded his head to indicate that yes, of course he knew what tides were. Lux sighed and rolled her eyes.

"Well the sun and the moon work together to make that happen. Without the moon, it just won't. Like that." She pointed towards the lake that was calm and ripple free. "It might seem like no big deal, but it is. The water temperature would drop which would harm the animals that live in it. The days would be shorter, only about 5 -6 hours, and the temperature would be totally different. It would be really bad, here and in your world too" she said gravely.

"Guess I just never thought about the moon that much before," Sebastien stared high into the sky with wonder. "I always just figured it was there to help us see in the dark at night time."

"Dragons have commanded the moon for a long, long time and it's a huge responsibility! And now my parents expect me to be able to learn to fly AND sing the song too, while I'm watching Nox all the time. You've seen how hard that job is." Lux let out a huge sigh and plopped down on the sand beside Sebastien. Clearly, watching her brother was as frustrating as it was for

Sebastien to watch Max.

He stood up and started walking around in circles, practicing balancing himself without falling over. He stopped when he realized something.

"Wait, you don't *know* the song already?? Aren't you supposed to be the one teaching me?" He looked at her confused, waiting for the answer.

"Umm.... well.... I kind of know it? I mean I almost totally know it? Like, my parents say it will just happen, and one time I'll be up so high, and I'll open my mouth to sing, and the words will just all come out, just like they're supposed to, just like it does for mom and dad, and I'll be the most amazing singer in the whole group!" Lux was talking very fast, trying to defend herself. A long sigh escaped her.

"I should probably tell you that I can't fly yet either." She was shuffling and wouldn't look him in the eyes, clearly embarrassed about the fact that she couldn't sing the song or fly yet. Sebastien bit his tongue to keep from freaking out about the situation. Making her feel worse wouldn't help anything.

"Okay let's take a minute and try to figure things out. We need to sing the song, we need to be flying when we do it right? Maybe I can fly now and I just don't know it!" He took a few awkward running steps forward and imagined himself soaring above the ground, majestically flapping his wings through the sky, just as glorious as the other dragons. He ran faster, lifted his wings and … *FLOOP*. Sebastien pushed himself off the ground and shook his head to clear it.

He said to himself *I CAN DO THIS*, and set off again running. Again he pictured himself soaring through the air, but he just couldn't figure out how to make his wings move the way they needed to to fly. *FLOOP*.

He got up and started pacing back and forth on the beach. They were on a time limit. They had to learn the song. They had to sing it while flying. Or maybe just from very high up.... He had caught sight of a cliff that looked pretty high but there was a path that led to it.

"Hey Lux! What if we cheat? Can we climb up to that cliff and sing from there? Would that be high enough?" He pointed up towards the cliff he'd spotted.

Lux thought about that for a bit. "Well, it's not how it's *supposed* to be done, but it's worth a try."

"Let's go up and we can practice on our way."

As they trudged along the winding path that led up to the cliff, Lux was humming a tune to herself and Sebastien was muttering to himself about how flying was dumb anyway.

CHAPTER 7
MARSHMALLOWS?

Max and Nox were having SO much fun playing together. They were leaping from rock to rock, jumping over branches on the ground, and they were even talking to one another, sort of. Max would point at a leaf and say “LEEF”, and the dragon baby would say “Nox”. Max would point at a rock and say “RAWK” and the dragon baby would say “Nox”. Max didn’t know why he kept saying ‘Nox’ but he thought it was funny!

After a while both boys were tired and ready for a break. Max hopefully asked if the dragon had anything he could eat. “Marshmallows??”

“Nox” said the dragon sadly, and shaking his head, and then hiccuped, and a small puff of fire came out of his nose.

Max jumped back when he saw the fire, and fell onto his bottom. His chin quivered, and a tear slowly rolled down his cheek. He felt exhausted, thirsty, and a little bit scared. He missed his sister and his brother, and his marshmallows. He looked over at Nox, and saw that he looked just as tired and scared as Max felt. He laid back on a pile of leaves on the ground and stared up at the canopy above them that the tree branches made. The small bit of light that filtered through the leaves reminded him of the rainbow shaped night light that hung on the wall in his bedroom at home. A giant yawn escaped him. Nox who was sprawled beside Max, arms behind his head, looking upwards too. Both boys enjoyed the stillness for a while.

Very quietly, Nox began to hum. It was a soft and slow tune, and Max enjoyed listening, because it made him feel a little less lost. He joined in after a while, smiling up at the trees above them as the humming got louder and turned into a song.

CHAPTER 8
MOON SONG

Selene and Solis were convinced that they would never find baby Nox. Their hurried pace had slowed down, and their faces told the story of their sadness. Selene was crying quietly, and Solis was muttering something to himself under his breath.

Elise was tired of walking, and was falling behind. Her legs were shorter than theirs, and she didn't think she'd ever walked this far in her whole life! Desperately she wanted to find the two little boys, and as soon as possible before her shoes started to get holes in them. Thoughts of good times playing with Max were running through her mind. All the times they'd pretended to be puppies, kitties, unicorns and dragons. All the times they'd eaten marshmallows together. All the times he'd given her one of his trademark giant hugs. Max was a delightful little brother (he bugged her WAY less often than Sebastien did, that's for sure) and she was really starting to miss him.

Now she was thinking of his cute little voice and the way he said her name, 'Leese', and how he would sing 'Tinkle tinkle leetle star' to her as they fell asleep. His voice was high pitched and babyish still (he was little after all) and she remembered it as though she had just heard him a minute before.

Wait a minute! She *was* hearing something, and it *did* sound like Max! Quickly she ran ahead to Selene and Solis, who were so busy being sad they hadn't heard it.

"Listen!" she said, grabbing both their arms at the same time, making them stop.

"I hear singing, and it sounds like Max!"

Both of the dragon's heads tilted to one side as they tried to hear what Elise was hearing, hopeful that she was right. A smile slowly grew on Selene's face and relief settled into her stance. Solis on the other hand looked confused.

"Is that your brother's voice? I hear two voices… is that Nox singing with him?" He turned slowly in a circle and tilted his head to the other side, listening harder to figure out whose voices he was hearing and where they were coming from. "Selene!" he said excitedly, "Could that be?! Is that our boy, singing!!?" Solis was practically dancing with delight as he hopped around on the little path. "We've never heard him sing!" he explained to Elise when he noticed her confused expression. "We keep trying to coax him, but we've never heard him sing!"

"Imagine, he hasn't sung a word his whole life, no matter how much we encouraged him, and now he is! He's singing the moon song we sing every night." Selene was dancing too, her arms fluttering about as she explained more of the story to Elise. "Where do you think they are? I think the singing is coming from that way." She was pointing ahead of them and to the right hand side of the path. It was hard to tell exactly as the voices were fading in and out.

The dragons quickly headed forward on the path, trying to see into the trees on the sides of the path. When they got near to where it seemed like the singing was coming from they realized the trees were so dense and thick they couldn't go very far off the path. Dragons are big!

"I can get them, I'm smaller than you." Elise said matter of factly. "Stay right here though, and listen for me to call you if I get turned around." It was a smart plan, since that is likely what had happened to the younger kids. They wandered off the path, got turned around and then didn't know the way back. She took a deep breath and gathered her courage, then set off into the woods.

She carefully stepped over tree roots and rocks, stopping every once in a while to listen for the singing voices and to make sure she was going in the right direction. The trees were so thick it was difficult to see anything around her except for tree trunks and branches. Ahead of her there was one big, low hanging branch blocking her way and she had to use both arms to move it aside. After she pushed it over and stepped past it she finally saw them. *Phew*.

"Max!" Elise yelled out, relieved. "We've all been so worried! Are you okay? You shouldn't wander away from us, ever again!" The words were pouring out of Elise, and her emotions were going from happy to mad to happy again. "Oh Max, I'm just glad I found you. Mom would have been so mad

at me for losing you!" Elise dropped down to her knees and Max ran into her arms for a classic giant hug that almost knocked her over. Nox was sitting, quietly watching their reunion, feeling hopeful that he would soon see his parents and sister again. He looked up with a tear stained face at Elise, who felt so sorry for the little sniffling guy.

"It's okay, baby dragon. You're safe

now. Do you want to come and see your parents?" Elise put an arm around him while he stood up, nodding. His sniffles stopped as they carefully made their way out of the forest. At one point Elise wasn't totally sure where to go, so she called out a little tune, repeating what the boys had been humming. Selene and Solis answered back with a similar few notes, and Nox's face lit up like a Christmas tree! He sang a few notes back to them, loudly and enthusiastically. They quickened their pace and soon burst through the dense trees, onto the path near to where the adult dragons were waiting.

Both parents let out a relieved cry and quickly ran to Nox's side. They hugged him, petted his cheek and told him how scared they had been. Nox just smiled, accepted all the love they were giving him, and said, 'Nox'. He was so incredibly happy to back with his family. The only dragon missing now was Lux.

CHAPTER NINE
COMMAND THE MOON

Their time was up.

One by one, the dragons flew out from behind the waterfall. They whizzed around in a circle, spiraling higher into the sky. Each nodded to the two dragons on the cliff, acknowledging their presence as they flew by. By this time these dragons assumed that the young dragons both knew the song and would join in with the rest, flying up into the sky to once again command the moon.

Lux could now sing the song, but had no confidence in herself to fly. Sebastien was starting to get the hang of flying (short

distances anyway) but hadn't yet been able to master the song. If only they could combine the skills they had, they'd feel confident in helping to lower the moon.

"Higher! Let's go higher!" Lux yelled to Sebastien as the dragons flew by. He followed her lead, running along the path higher up the cliff until they reached the very top.

Sebastien was more scared than he had ever been. Four grown dragons were expecting him to jump off this cliff and fly with them. Looking over at Lux he saw his fear mirrored in her face. She was so nervous she was trembling, and looked like she might puke. *I have to show her she can do it*, he thought to himself. *I have to show her it's possible, and if I can do it, of course she can do it.* He closed his eyes, took and enormous breath in, he started running to the edge of the cliff.

"Fly!" Sebastien yelled to Lux, as he leapt

off the cliff to join the other dragons.

"Sing!" she yelled to him as she began the song while watching him with astonishment and admiration.

It was taking all of his concentration to work his back muscles in the way they needed to, to make his wings flap in unison. His forehead was scrunched as he focused on staying high in the sky and not falling. He couldn't believe he had done it! He had leapt off the edge of a cliff believing he could fly, and now he actually was!

It was beginning to get easier...in fact, Sebastien was starting to enjoy it. Soon he found that he didn't have to think about his movements quite so much. It was time for him to try singing. He tried to remember the song Lux was singing on the way up the mountain. He was kind of, sort of singing the right words, and it was kind of, sort of on key, but since he wasn't actually a real dragon, his voice just wasn't as good as the others.

"Lux!! You have to help me! I'm not good enough. You have to fly! You can do it, I know you can!" Sebastien yelled down to her as he flew in circles around the edge of the cliff. He could see the scared look on her face, and he realized he needed a backup plan– he didn't think Lux was going to be able to fly. Desperately he looked around, hoping that the other dragons would be able to offer a suggestion, but they were all deep in concentration while they sang.

The moon wasn't falling and the water was still completely calm, which could only mean the song wasn't working. He looked around at the faces of the other dragons. Their eyes filled with worry as they glanced back at him. Panicked, Sebastien tried to sing the song louder, but only made him start to wobble. He thought he would fall out of the sky. He just couldn't do it!

Just as Sebastien was about to cry out

in desperation, a whoosh of air blew past him. He turned his head to see Lux flying in the air beside him with a giant smile on her face. He could tell that her wings were not quite as strong as the adult dragons, but she had found a rhythm and was holding her spot in the circle.

She nodded her large head at him and began to sing. Her voice was magical and pure. For a moment he just listened to her, enjoying the deep tone of her voice. He added his voice once again to the group.

The moon started to move. Slowly, it began to sink lower in the sky. The other dragons looked approvingly toward them and continued their song with a renewed energy. With Lux and Sebastien the dragon singing, they were sure to correct last night's mistake.

Sebastien felt another whoosh of air blow past him. He looked over to see Selene and Solis, strong and true, staring approvingly at their daughter while they joined in the song. Their voices held great joy and happiness, and they added a rich, deep tone to the song. Very quickly now, the moon fell. Within a minute it had sunk past the horizon and the daylight began peaking up and filling the sky with light. The light from the sun grew brighter and more brilliant as it climbed higher into the sky. It was the most beautiful sunrise any of them had ever seen.

Sebastien wasn't quite sure what he was supposed to do at this point. The song was over and the group was holding formation in the air, just above the lake, which had started to ebb and flow again. One by one, the adult dragons left their place in the circle and flew past Lux and Sebastien. Each one seemed to convey their gratitude towards the two new singers in a different way. One dragon bowed his head as he flew past, another snorted a bit of fire, and another winked!

After all of the other dragons had paid their respects, Selene, Solis, Lux and Sebastien flew slowly down to the ground at the bottom of the mountain, landing next to Elise, Max and Nox. Sebastien grinned a massive dragony smile, full of pride and extremely relieved to see his brother safe and found.

"Max!!" he exclaimed, as he rushed towards the little guy.

CHAPTER TEN
HOME TIME

Max's heart raced with fear at the sight of his brother, the dragon. He eyes grew wide and he began to tremble as Sebastien moved towards him. Max didn't know what to think of it all. He caught sight of the spikes coming out of Sebastien's back, and the forked tail, and ran to Elise. He pressed his face close to her body, squeezing his eyes shut while holding on to her tightly.

The unknown, gleaming purple dragon dropped to its knees a little ways away from Max. It stared into Max's eyes and spoke softly to him.

"It's okay, it's me, Sebastien, your brother. I'm just… a dragon now. I'm really glad Elise found you, you scared us again!" Sebastien stayed still. Max looked at the dragon, studying his eyes, before venturing forward.

Could this really be my brother, thought Max as he gazed deeper into Sebastien's wide-set eyes. *It is!* With a sigh of acceptance, he walked forward into the dragon's arms and gave him a very big hug.

"You big dragon, Sebby?" Max asked him, using the nickname he used since the name Sebastien was so hard for him to say.

Sebastien laughed and nodded. Yup, he was a big dragon alright! Flying had been amazing, but walking around with the big tail was starting to get annoying.

Selene and Solis were telling Lux how proud they were that she had finally flown and been able to sing the song and Lux was glowing with the praise. They turned towards the human children and Sebastien.

"You kids coming here to our land was a magical wonder," Solis said to them. "Selene and I haven't been singing that well for a while now, because we've been so worried about our kids! Nox couldn't sing and Lux couldn't fly. We were starting to think the dragon's song would be in danger, if they didn't learn soon. There are no other dragon children right now, and a few of the dragons in our group are getting older. They won't be able to sing very much longer. Your arrival here created events that we never would have wanted– it was so scary to lose Nox– but it was the best thing that could have happened! Thank you. Thanks to all of you children. We will tell the tale of this day for many years."

When Solis finished speaking, he turned towards his children and drew them close for an awkward dragon hug. Selene walked over to Sebastien and put her hand on his shoulder.

"Thank *you* especially, Sebastien. Without your encouragement and friendship I'm not sure Lux would have ever been brave enough to fly. I think she was inspired by your courage. I truly appreciate what you've done today for my children. My guess is that your mother will be wanting you back home with her soon. Do you know how to return home?"

Do I know home to get home? Sebastien wondered to himself. He looked around for the dragon tooth that had brought them to this amazing place. *Perhaps if the tooth brought us here, it can bring us back home.* He spotted it lying partially covered by some leaves a little ways away, probably dropped there when he became a dragon and fell on his butt!

"Yah, we're good." he told her. "I'm glad you got your baby back. Elise! Max! Say goodbye and then let's go." Sebastien turned to Lux and suddenly felt shy. "Thanks for teaching me how to fly, and to sing like that. It was really cool."

Lux nodded her head, and agreed with him. A wide grin spread across her face. "Yah, it really was. Maybe I'll see you again sometime." She gave him a small wave, and then waved and said goodbye to Elise and Max. "Try to stay close to your brother and sister, little guy," she said affectionately, and patted Max's head. She took off into the sky, happily heading up to the clouds. "See you around!" she called. She flew higher and higher, finally turning as she swooped straight into the waterfall.

Nox and Max gave each other a little hug and a smile and then parted. Elise ran to Selene and Solis and gave them each a big hug. Of course Max had to give them each a hug too. Then finally the kids were ready to leave.

The kids all stood near to one another, and waved and saying goodbye to the dragons one more time. Sebastien picked up the tooth and blew into it again. Just as it had done before, a brilliant light poured out of the tooth and blotted out everything around them.

CHAPTER 11
COURAGE

The three children opened their eyes to find themselves in their basement once again. Blinking slowly a few times, they looked around to regain their sense of surroundings.

Sebastien was no longer a dragon, he was back to being a 9 year old boy, tall and blonde and swaying a bit from side to side.

"You okay?" Elise asked. She knew from experience turning into a human again came with a weird, dizzying feeling. "Give it a minute, you'll get used to not having a tail soon." She was trying to keep her giggles to herself, but he heard them anyway.

"Did that really happen??!" he said to

her and Max in a small voice. He had been turned into a dragon, learned to sing a magical song AND learned to fly. What a day!

"Look!" Max yelled and pointed to Sebastien's neck, startling his siblings. He now had a dark crystal necklace, very similar to Elise's, hanging around his neck. So that was cool.

"Kids, dragons, whatever you are! Time to fly up now!"

They remembered that they'd been playing dragons before they'd discovered the tooth and had a laugh at their mom's attempt at a joke. If only she knew.

Max went running upstairs at top speed. He loved bath time because their mom always made it really fun with food colouring and baking soda. She called it 'magic powder' and it was really fun to play with.

"Hey, you were really brave to leap off that cliff. How'd you know you could fly?" Elise asked her big brother.

"I didn't. I started off sure that I couldn't... there was just no way! I mean, those wings were really hard to work. But then I looked at Lux, and at how she was so sure she couldn't do it. I just knew that I had to fly. I had to prove to her that it could be done. I remember I took a deep breath, closed my eyes and JUMPED. Next thing I knew I was flying. I took a chance, and it worked. Good thing, right?" he laughed a bit, thinking about the alternative.

"Yup, good thing. I sure wouldn't want to explain what happened to mom and dad. No way." Elise paused for a moment, thinking about the unbelievable journeys they'd had. "I wonder where we'll go to next time, if there is a next time?" Elise stood still, looking thoughtfully at the suitcase, as Sebastien tucked the tooth into a little pocket sewn into the side.

Sebastien poked her in the side. “Not sure, but I hope I get to fly again soon!” They made their way up the stairs, talking non-stop about the possibility of fairies, elves and wonderlands.

~ABOUT THE AUTHORS~

Laurie Wright- Laurie is a speaker, author, and educator who is passionate about helping children increase their positive self-talk and improve their mental health. Laurie speaks to parents, teachers, has given a TEDx talk, created resources and has written 2 books, all to further the cause of improving the self-esteem of our children. Laurie is a huge advocate for children's mental health and works every day to improve the way we interact with kids, to help them learn to handle all of their emotions

Jennifer Dale Stables- B.F.A, B.Ed.

Illustrator and contributing author, Jennifer Dale Stables, grew up in the small prairie town of Bow Island, Alberta. A former classroom teacher, Jennifer has dedicated her artistic endeavors to creating artwork and illustrations for children. Through her business, Jenny Dale Designs, she creates whimsical artwork and writes poetry to accompany each one of her lovable creations. Dragon's Song is Jennifer's tenth published book.

Printed in Germany
by Amazon Distribution
GmbH, Leipzig

17273346R00061